Lapse Americana

Also by Benjamin Myers

Elegy for Trains, Village Books Press, 2010

Lapse Americana

Benjamin Myers

The New York Quarterly Foundation, Inc.
New York, New York

NYQ Books™ is an imprint of The New York Quarterly Foundation, Inc.

The New York Quarterly Foundation, Inc.
P. O. Box 2015
Old Chelsea Station
New York, NY 10113

www.nyqbooks.org

First Edition

Set in New Baskerville

Layout and Design by Raymond P. Hammond
Cover Layout and Design by Corey Lee Fuller

Library of Congress Control Number: 2013932935

ISBN: 978-1-935520-71-9

Lapse Americana

Acknowledgments

My gratitude is due first to God, triune and eternal. Secondly, I would like to thank my wife, Mandy, for her support and patience. Thirdly, thank you to Raymond Hammond and everyone else at the *New York Quarterly* and NYQ Books.

I am grateful to the editors, staffs, patrons, and readers of the following journals, in which the poems listed below first appeared.

Borderlands: Texas Poetry Review: "Loss"
Chiron Review: "Mysterious God" and "The Tardy Ones"
Christianity and Literature: "French Press"
Concho River Review: "A Friend's Divorce"
Cybersoleil: "Talking to my Racist Friend"
Devil's Lake: "Pep Talk"
DMQ Review: "Odin" and "Trampoline"
elimae: "Agent of Infinite Regression"
Foundling Review: "Going Far"
Iron Horse Literary Review: "Cedars" and "Pastoral"
Mayo Review: "Service Station"
New Plains Review: "The City Dump"
New York Quarterly: "Spook House"
Nimrod: "Agincourt"
Numinous: "What Hamlet Got Wrong"
Pedestal Magazine: "Notes from a Time Traveler"
Plainsongs: "Deep Fork"
poetrybay: "Oracle"
Rock and Sling: "Class Outside"
Salamander: "A Production of Hamlet" and "None of This"
San Pedro River Review: "Wanderlust"
Tar River Poetry: "A Family"
Westview: "The Books of the Dead" and "An Urgent Message To Li Po"

"On my Thirty-fifth Birthday" and "The Circus Comes to Lincoln County" first appeared in *Ain't Nobody That Can Sing Like Me: An Anthology of New Oklahoma Writing* (Mongrel Empire Press, 2010). Thanks to Jeanetta Calhoun Mish. "Tornado" first appeared in the

"Walt's Corner" column in the *Long Islander* newspaper. Thanks to George Wallace. "Summer Work" appeared in the anthology *Elegant Rage* (Village Books Press, 2012), in honor of the Woody Guthrie Centennial. Thanks to Dorothy Alexander.

This book was greatly improved by time spent with it at the Colrain Poetry Manuscript Conference, and I am grateful to Joan Houlihan and Henry Israeli for advice offered there. I am grateful as well to the other conference participants, especially Kim Garcia, J. J. Pena, and Michael Rotenberg-Schwartz.

Amanda J. Bradley and Ashley Martin offered much useful advice on poems and on the manuscript. Nathan Brown, Ken Hada, Devey Napier, and my mother, Anna Myers, offered much needed encouragement throughout the writing of this book, as did my colleagues at Oklahoma Baptist University, especially Anne Hammond, Karen Youmans, and Carolyn Cole.

"French Press" is for Andrew Armond. "Good Friday at the Alamo" is for Bill Hagen. "Once on the Aegean" is for Brad McLelland. "Going Far" is for Jason Tillis.

"Notes from a Time Traveler" is for David Strain, with whom I first read Yeats.

for
Paul Myers,
American Poet
(1943-1999)

Contents

iii

iv

coda

prelude

Two Ravens perch on Odin's shoulder to whisper all they have discovered. They are called Thought and Memory.

Gylfaginning of the Prose Edda, chapter 38

There is no remembrance of former things; neither shall there be any remembrance of things that are to come with those that shall come after.

Ecclesiastes 1:11

SPOOK HOUSE

The first I heard of Dante
was at the county fair when I was ten,
Dante's Inferno slashed in red on a black
trailer at the bottom of the hill
where they showed the livestock.
It was surrounded by little lights
like the blinking eyes of the damned
and booths with stacks of old-fashioned
milk bottles: two dollars for
three throws and you could win
a mirror painted with the rebel
flag or with a half-naked lady,
or with a naked lady half-wrapped
in the rebel flag. I wanted

to go on the Ferris Wheel,
for the way it turned above
the noise and the smell
of manure and funnel cakes,
how it reminded me
of a queen I saw
in a movie once, raising
her head to meet the eye
of the executioner.

My friends wanted the thrill
of Dante's trailer, where shrieks
and groans from a cone speaker
mixed with bleats drifting
down from sheep on the hill.

This was the summer
Nick O'Hare's cousin
killed himself
after graduation, and a drought
set in that left the earth
cracked and flaked like old paint.

But there wasn't a war then.

I stood in line looking out
over cars parked on dead grass,
their jagged rows like gravestones,
two big crows perched
on the utility pole at the center.

Years later, there is a copy
of *La Commedia* on my desk
while I write this, and two
more editions on the shelf,
but I'm thinking of how we entered
the *Inferno* two at a time
in little cars on a greasy track,
how a bar lowered across our laps
and two black doors swung open
as we watched our friends
before us disappear around a dark curve.

THE CITY DUMP

John Black started digging a grave the morning
his wife ran off to Tulsa with the insurance adjuster;
he dug it by the bare mimosa
overhanging the right-of-way in front
of their low ranch house by the highway,
and he had to chop through sandstone and clay,
hauling up rock bare-headed in the sun
until evening came and he laid himself
down in the hole for two days, watching
the swollen moon chase a frail, lemon sun
across that rectangular patch of sky.
The third day his brother came
and sat beside the grave in a plastic
lawn chair, talked about livestock
and fishing until John, to prove
a point about casting into brush, rose
to get his gear.

           Now he's here, his pickup
next to Will Miller, who never married
and lives in a house he built from salvage
beside the dirt speedway, lying awake
Friday nights and listening to the cars go
around and around while he thinks of waves
washing over stones on the Pacific shore.

And there's Dave Fox, who went to Vietnam
and came back to teach geometry,
thirty-five years, daily translating the torn children
in burned-out villages
into mathematical precision,
abstracting from the tall and shifting grass
the triangle and the parallel line,
eating perfectly halved peanut-butter
sandwiches in the run-down teachers' lounge.

They are pushing back against the growing junk
of winter—pine needles, busted refrigerators,
broken hoses in all sizes, balding tires—
though they know full well that each blessed year
brings it back and that a man can never
stay ahead for long.

        And sometimes they dream—
each of them—of the mounds growing beyond
their control, breaking like dark waves
of a midnight sea over their low rows
of houses, over the farms and stalled-out
tractors,

        but, for now, they are at the dump,
upright in the back of pickup trucks, cleaning
out long beds with sideways sweep of brown,
rounded work boots, as they kick out the remnants
of their haul, one knee each rising, falling
in a crooked jig above brush piles and sacks of trash,
where the honeyed sunlight drips over truck
hoods onto gravel and a cardinal
is calling from beyond the chain-link fence,
and it is spring,

        and the men are dancing.

SOMETIMES I DREAM OF THE ANALOG WORLD

Sometimes I am sitting by a large window typing
a letter to you. One thing touches

another. There are birds singing without
zeros and ones in their voices, but you are

a faraway city where people are
still completely alone in their cars.

Later, in the dream, I will call you
with wires between us all the way

over the slow breathing and deeper sleeping
shoulders of the middle of this country.

But I never dream of the friend
who came to sit up all night

with me after my father died,
or of how we played Dad's Edith

Piaf records over and over until dawn,
watching the turntable sway its French hips

while we smoked cheap cigars. I am talking
about mediation, how we suck it in and spit it out.

Back in this sometimes dream there are shaking
red lines on my television where a woman like you

is buying a bunch of bananas
and paying with cash. I turn

the painted chrome knob and go
outside, where the sun is its very own yellow.

THE CIRCUS COMES TO LINCOLN COUNTY

In a sequined leotard
and opaque tights
a girl stands in front of the sons
and daughters of Baptist farmers.
She has twelve white pigeons
on a revolving wheel,
flapping their wings to rotate,
and the crowd applauds
lightly, the sound of cattle
thudding slowly through the grass.

There is one ring,
a cyclops eye of reddish-brown
earth, that sees, over the course
of an hour,
one lion, two tigers, a clown,
five acrobats, and a man
in an ape suit,

but the act we love is a juggler
named Angel,
a small and dandelion kind of kid,
who spins five rings above his head
like a universe of phantom Saturns.

When we leave, not only the children
are looking back
over shoulders into the shadowed
tent where Angel
is lighting his cigarette.

AGINCOURT

My neighbor's son is jumping
from a helicopter into a field of poppies

that might explode. The father, proud
and worried, tells me about it one morning

as I water the wilting flowers
in front of our house and he stands

with a newspaper bag and a cup of coffee.
The elderly lady across the street comes out in her bathrobe

to smoke a cigarette and clip her roses, and I
ask myself if I could die to save her right to stand there

with her paper-white legs out-paling the morning
sun. In church they ask the soldiers to stand, and the pews

become a time-lapse forest around me, redwoods
straight up on all sides while I sit low as a rotted fern.

I don't know what I believe about this war,
and I hear Branagh's King Henry declare that I

will hold my manhood cheap. My manhood is middle
aged and nearsighted and has read far too many books.

The national guard convoys rattle the windows
of our little house when they roll down Main Street.

What can I say to those others, no different from me, really,
filing off into Afghanistan, like letters mailed to God?

SUMMER WORK

There is a sky like sharpened bone
over the trailer home
with tinfoil in all the windows,
where I wait while my foreman
smokes weed from a metal pipe.

We were to start early—
already it's hot—
but I had to pick him up
again. He won't go
until he's high. Outside
beneath the mangy
mimosa over the dirt
drive, a dog on a chain
whines against the heat
loudly enough to be heard
inside above the box fan.

The big boss will have finished
with the bobcat and is waiting
for our shovels to even the dig,
where the concrete will be poured,
where the pool will be lined
with cool blue plastic, behind
the house we never go into.

My foreman is a screw-up
named Joe, with a suspended
license, a trailer on the margins,
and a married girlfriend
who smokes like a damp log.

He is sitting on the spotted brown carpet,
leaning back against a couch,
pipe in one hand, lighter in the other,
and he's telling me about his first
year out of high school—expelled,

not graduated—how he'd actually get
up early, since he didn't have to,
and walk off into the aimless housing
of Edmund, Oklahoma in the 70's. He's taking
a drag and staring at the wall. He's telling
me how he would steal motorcycles,

how he would move through the early dark,
trying each garage door with his fingers
until he felt one give. He's telling me
how he would raise it just
enough and crawl beneath
on his belly. He's remembering
how the concrete always felt warm,
how his eyes would adjust in the dark
garage, how if there was no bike
he would crawl back out, how if there was

he would hotwire it quick as cussing,
throw the door up, and burn
off down the street. He's telling me how
he would spend the day just riding
and riding, finally humming out along the lake
shore, the vast and manmade reservoir
beyond the city limits. He's telling me
how he'd walk the bike along the frail
rail bridge, rubber tires rubbing over wooden
slats, to a gap in the rusty trellis, how
he'd push the bike over the edge, the headlamp
on so he could watch the circle of light
sink into the murk below.

TRAMPOLINE

                    My father hauled junk,
when there was no other work, lugging
broken remnants of skipped out tenants:
garbage bags of sheet-thin clothes, bits
of broken baby furniture.
                             Our only asset
was empty space. He dumped the stuff
behind our barn, a ghost
town in boom with broken jars of pickled
okra, lawn mowers missing wheels,
a row of lidless washers hoarding
rain,
          and, once, a chest of drawers stuffed
with translucent white nightgowns, the top
drawer open, dropping pale lace petals
into the wind.

                 I thought nothing
in Lincoln County still worked. At school
I took my beatings from an older boy dropped
back into our grade
                   and went home
prowling behind the barn with a lead pipe,
swinging down on vacant screens of dead
televisions, to feel a jolt run up my arm,
to hear the crack.
                We cleared the dark
bones of a burned-out trailer, burdening
the flatbed truck with charred two-by-fours
and aluminum siding. My father's cigarette dropped
white ash on blackened concrete.
                     I loaded
a mattress burned to bare springs and browned
by flame, knew the trailer was home
to the boy who beat me.

          We all knew his father
was a drunk. Some said he torched the house
in rage, others that he fell asleep smoking.

                                        I confess
to not caring much and to dragging that night
those mattress springs from the pile, brutal and—God
help me—happy as I jumped.

LICE

Beside the pink sink shaped like a seashell, my mother
is picking through my hair for tiny bugs.
She keeps one hand beneath my chin to hold
me angled toward the light above the sink.
The same is happening at other houses,
dirty ones and poor, where the father is
all fist, not kind like mine. I must have caught
the bugs at school from kids with scabby
heads, red like fields of turned mud beneath
the scraggly grass: for instance, Leroy Hoover
who came to school in T-shirts, even when
it snowed, his bandy arms flailing like flagella in the halls.
Tomorrow, I'll stand with him beneath fluorescent lights
to be inspected before we can return to class,
where other kids will watch us walk in late,
staring from their little desks and plastic chairs.
I try to think I'm not like him, but here, tonight, mostly
I just like the feeling of my mother's fingers in my hair.

CEDARS

They are not native to this place
but have rushed the grassy hill,
an infantry in spiky green. Go back
a century and the prairie was
unbroken, Donne's *gold to airy thinness beat*,
but now the extension man
says we have lost 3 million acres
of our herd's dominion.

From my old bedroom window,
I could trace the seeds' progression,
watch the cedars march
over the pasture and beyond
the barbed wire at its back.

One December my father
asked the rancher who owned
all the land around us
for permission to cut a few cedars
to sell as Christmas trees.
The rancher said he wished
we'd take them all, and we took
all we could. Rising early to a dry,
cold day and a wind like fire
over the prairie, we waded
into a morning tide of scrub oak
and eastern red cedar,
where we took turns with the saw,
one bending to cut, the other straight up
with an arm through the biting green
to steady the trunk
until the stump let it loose.

We sold enough to make the ride
home merry in the darkening air
and to cheer the little kitchen

where my mother laid ground
meat in a well-greased pan
while my sisters set the table.

Outside the wind
ripped through the ragged
arms of the cedars,
their red and shaggy roots
deep in alien clay.

JUMP CUT

From the lost civilization
  of the 70's,
    only fragments remain:

the chipped and flaking moon skidding
  along inside the car window,
    my father singing "Rocket Man"

from the front seat,
  shadows of streetlamps passing
    in bars over my lap.

When I was four, our house
  burned down. Of that house
    I remember

only bare plank flooring,
  a train of wooden blocks I ran
    in circles around me.

I know I'm not
  the only kid ever to lose
    a decade.

Still, do you know
  what a jump cut is,
    the most famous being

in Godard's *Breathless,*
  as they ride
    in the car, a seismic

rub of two moments
  hard-edged against
    each other, time

as tectonic event,
  but another being perhaps
    that me and this?

  Of the whole decade I remember
    most the sound of water
      running in the cold tile bathroom.

SERVICE STATION

Three pumps stand with their hands
in their pockets out front, waiting
for scraps of breeze to tumble
in over the yellow grass of August.

This is a memory: my grandmother's
blue sedan crossing the dark
hose stretched like a garter
snake sunning itself on the hot concrete:

strange snake that sings in two chimes
quick as crickets to call the man, father
of a classmate, in coveralls from his small
black and white television.

Then the cleaning of the windshield,
the movement like a typewriter's roll
across the glass, the attendant
flicking his wrist at each line's end.

Taking the tire gage like a physician's
thermometer from his chest pocket,
he bends toward the heat that is
bouncing from white concrete. There is much

wear on our tires, and the windshield
is spider-webbed with tiny cracks.
We sit with windows down
and watch him raise the hood until all we see

ahead is a new sky of faded blue
flecked with clouds of primer gray.

LAND RUN

This Land Run Day, I'm inviting
all my Indian friends over for a barbecue.
I'm giving them little plastic tent stakes,
inviting them to claim pieces of my yard.

Our town elders have lined up children
in the park, little girls in prairie-flower
dresses with bonnets tied beneath their chins,
boys in overalls, some with boots: the costume
or imagined costume of their pioneer ancestors.
One girl's father has made a covered wagon
from a lawn-cart by stretching a bed sheet
over five hoops of wire. She pulls
it with a plastic handle.

In the real land run, they came
also by train, the Santa Fe line sagging
down from Kansas so loaded that men
sat on the roof and hung out the windows,
jumping from the slowing train
like fleas from a shaking dog
as it shuddered into Guthrie.

Whole cities were raised in a day: what was
buffalo wallow is now
my backyard drainage problem,
puddle water bulging
with mosquito larvae,
no buffalo shag to soak up
the meager rain.

GOING FAR

We were not doomed
enough to be beautiful.
So they sentenced us
to ride around in cars,

abandoned satellites falling
through an endless orbit,
maple keys twisting
in a circular wind.

From blue to infinite
blue runs the main
street of our little town,

atop the hill, a seven
block stretch of 66.

The bored teenage years,
on long, thin Saturday afternoons,
we would drive the highway
as far as half our gas money
would take us and stare
down the line of road

until the distant sky
appeared a lake, the bank of cloud
like mountains beyond
rising to a higher sky.

Those nights, folded in the thick
arms of sleep we would
dream the dreams of birds
heading north again,
taking their wings and an outbound
wind to ride.

There was a fire
in my chest back then:

the burn is gone,
but the light remains.

TORNADO

Toward evening the clouds began
circling each other like dogs.
A light like the golden skin
of the sun itself fell
steady as rain before the rain
and puddled between round bales
uncollected in the pasture.

Then the utility poles
were a row of broken teeth
up the highway to town,

and once again
the ordinary light.

A PRODUCTION OF HAMLET

In Delacroix's famed version of the grave-
yard scene—which I cut from the program of
the opera by Thomas, crammed inside

a cheap black frame, and hung above my desk—
it is the man who digs the grave who holds
the skull and not the melancholy Dane.

He stands waist deep in open trench and grips
the dead man's head above his own as if
to rise together from the earth, some bits

of which are clinging to his sunburned chest.
His friend sits on the graveside like a dock,
his feet dropped in the waters of the grave,

his back to us. The nobles stand above.
And Hamlet, even wrapped in black, seems too
refined for death, his hands two handkerchiefs

of linen white, his face a candle's flame
at noon. And though I love the pouty Dane,
I also love the hint the painter gives

that only those who work with earth can know
the forceful claim the dirt has on our soul's
poor mute companion. Looking up, they seem

to ask, *how will you shake the hand of death
with palm as clean as that?*

CUBIST SPRING

1.
April is a dog, wet and shuddering, come limping in after hard
      winter. The last ice storm took out half the trees in town, left the rest

carved at odd angles, so when finally they bloomed it was cubist
      spring, spastic bouquets bursting color up one side of trunk: Bradford

Pear lopsided in white explosion, Redbud breaking itself open in pink
      splotches dripping against corrugated tin of auto body shop and sky.

2.
Bill Miller's wife won't let him
smoke in the house, so he stands
on his front porch watching rain
walk up the street to lay down in puddles
on his front lawn. Drops are blowing onto
the tips of his boots; he sees moisture
spread across leather like shadow
of cloud moving on grass, thinks
back two decades, their first
apartment, its little kitchen,
dishwasher rolled up to the sink,
attached by hose to the faucet.
He remembers his young wife
in the kitchen looking out
at a wall across the alley, her thoughts
a box of coins at the bottom of the sea.
Bill has come home from a class
on engineering, thinking how he would
like to be a painter. He's come to tell
her about streaks of light climbing
off water, up the river bridge
like vines. He sees worry in her hands
beneath scalding water. They
took a mortgage like a tumor beneath
the skin. Their son has left
for college. Bill stands

on the porch smoking,
thinking of his father leaving
for work before dawn, little beads
of bacon grease in his beard, cup
of black coffee balanced on the dashboard
of the truck. He puts out his cigarette.

Something inside him is exploding like firecrackers in a coke
        bottle: uneven, bright, and painful like all the trees of that cubist spring.

HOW DID YOU SPEND THE WAR

today? I had
a cup of coffee and learned
I can take off like a helicopter
but fly like a plane.

The wild daffodils tilting at the river's edge,
an old man limping, one hand on a boy's shoulder.

Just think: Bob was brush-hogging
on the right-of-way
when the semi hit him, and so
his son went to art school
after all. After all

the noise of the party boat,
only ripples of its wake
nudging
the grassy shore.

Yet, from up here the unholy
sound of traffic is a
bit like a bee, stunned
by a sudden frost and dying
at the windowsill.

I'm sometimes afraid I've never really lived.

Nevertheless, the living thing is out there in the darkness.
The living thing is out there

still.

ON MY THIRTY-FIFTH BIRTHDAY

Rambling through the rooms
in which fathers
wander—picking up worry
and setting it down, picking
up love—I meet
my own father, fresh
from his cancer

and follow him through
afternoon rooms
of unmoving light,
to a place where
I am seven years old
and he is fixing our neighbor's
water heater, bending
to it like a ranch-hand
to the birthing cow.
I am holding the wrench, and he
is teaching me that a man
can fool a machine into working
just a little longer.

Further back
there is a screen-door:
already he has passed through.
I am standing
with my toes against the threshold, straining
to see through wire mesh
while he lingers
at the edge of a dark line of trees,
waving for me to follow.

NONE OF THIS

You are eight years old and on the parallel eye
of the tire swing, hovering at the end of three chains over

your grandmother's yard. You spin the eye to twist the chains
and stare up into their collapsing pyramid, spiraled.

Above you two crows sit on the cottonwood branch,
two dark sores on the pale of leprous skin, a soft wound

where three chains bite into the wood. Light is
tumbling through the definite leaves

down the chains and onto your forearms. You are
thinking about nothing. What was there

before there was something? You have not read
Milton yet or Hesiod or Genesis. You try

to picture nothing but see only whiteness. Is
that nothing? No, it is whiteness. You try

again and see this time only blackness, which is
blackness. Through the wide open

kitchen window you hear your mother talking.
You see in the corner of your eye an aunt

at the kitchen table subdivided by the screen
in the window into hundreds of tiny squares.

She is drinking coffee. It is early. There are more
birds in the tree above you. It is not yet

hot. None of this is nothing.

ODIN

My friend is forgetting
me, his mind a tree blooming
with bagworm, the gloss slipping
from once green leaves.

I visit his study
at home, books piled
in ruins around us. His wife
brings us coffee (to grow
cold in its ceramic walls),
while he searches my face
like an engine straining to turn.

She tells me later
how she found him
in the breakfast cereal
aisle, transfixed before
hundreds of cartoon eyes,
and how she locks the door
at night to keep him from looking
for some ghostly home.

Thought and Memory are two
crows. Each dawn Odin
lets them loose to search
the earth for what is there,
black wings painting
frost in long strokes
of shadow.

The old man waits
in the cold throne room.
The crows will come again
never.

THOSE DARKENED NEIGHBORHOODS

My friend, you are watching the power
failure from the high vantage point
of your standing body, looking out
over the successively darkening neighborhoods
of your mind.
It begins with where you live
now, the low brick homes and lawns
without sidewalks falling
from the lighted cliff into darkness.

Now you can see the distant lights
of a campus where you taught
for thirty years blink out
classroom by classroom as colleagues
retired, moved-on, or dead
wander aimlessly from their darkened offices.
Other campuses follow it
into the rushing black:
that state school, with its tan
and gray brick, where you took
your first position;
the graduate school where you were
the most promising young scholar
rushing through the colonnade,
a stack of books under your long arms;
the undergraduate place where you sang
barefoot with a guitar on the grassy mall.
There is not a campus left in the light.

Now there goes a scruffy row of houses,
like a grizzled beard, darkened down
to the corner where you worked the little grocery;

and the neighborhood where you followed
the line of dawn, delivering papers
up and down the brightening streets,

has reversed itself to move
back into the darkness,

which has just arrived at the borders
of your childhood. It is creeping
across the empty lot where you played
ball all summer and is now covering the walls
of the little congregational church. See,
it is pausing to breathe

at the crumbling concrete stoop
where your young mother
has cupped her hand to her mouth
and is calling your name.

A FIELD IN AUGUST

for Friends Dead in the Last Century

The long, sun-blonde and moving grass
in which I stand presents to me
a picture of last century,
this breathing plain the mass

of years a score removed from Christ.
This pasture's like a place we left
some people whom we love, bereft
of shade that once sufficed

to cool a summer afternoon.
And looking back into that field
we see among the blades concealed
the eyes and hands we lost too soon.

Now night has settled like a flock
of blackbirds on that yellow spread,
and we must walk beyond our dead
'till rustling grass obscures their talk.

THOUGHT AND MEMORY

1.
Round bales in a green field
after rain,
one pitch crow flying low
between them.

2.
Camped by a frozen
creek, I smoke
a crudely carved pipe.

Two crows have settled
to pick gravel on the opposite
bank.

I am beginning
to forget
my father's house.

3.
Leaving the sick man's home,
we notice
the feet of crows
have left
little sketches
of lightning in the dust.

APOSTROPHE

I've tried to be your friend,
you bastard, Time.
That day I held your hands,
the hours, and sat on the gray
rocks by the gray
river, counting the northward
geese dotting the fog:
that was me reaching out.

But then, just when I'm trying to learn
French, you go running
off with the physicist
before I've even mastered
the subjunctive.

Do you ever let anyone master the subjunctive?

When I see your sister,
Death, downtown, I complain
about you,
but she is so preoccupied
these days herself
and only shakes her dark braids
before hurrying off
into a crowd of Danish tourists.

And you go on,
poking a bony finger
into every good meal I've ever tried to eat,
asking *are you going to finish that?*
Can I clear that plate?
Is this the day you die?

Oh, you must think it funny,
re-clothing the trees each year
before stripping them naked again:
this mockery is sick. I'm sure
Dr. Freud would tell you about it,
if you hadn't eaten his face.

ANCHISES

In the room of buzzing white,
      air-conditioning
      hums its mechanics
into the still, chilled silence;
      students stare at me,

sea-eyed and trembling, the book
      hanging wide open
      like a bat pre-flight
from my shaking, chalk-marked hand.
      Best of fathers, he

has died once again this year.
      We have followed him
      through three books—his old
bones borne through the hungry
      flames of Troy,

the sea journey long as life,
      the mistaken starts—
      and now we are here
in this quiet room. They scuff
      their feet on carpet.

Someone coughs. Beyond the door
      their lunch is waiting.
      They do not realize:

Anchises, Anchises, Anchises, you are dead.

THE FORGOTTEN PAGES

In early summer we sleep with the windows open, and I am awakened one predawn by a rustling of pages like cicadas. The house has been filled with the leaves of books, torn from their bindings, each with one edge ragged like a field of high grass dusted with snow.

I shuffle through the white, thigh deep, to the kitchen and pour my breakfast cereal. Bits of *War and Peace* come fluttering out like doves. When I add the milk, the Russian names float away from their verbs.

In the study, I find the pages cover my desk, now like ash over an Italian village. They must be reread to be re-forgotten. I begin with a few pages from a friend's dissertation, little Foucaults and Derridas swarming all over. Then I move on to the page beneath, which is Yuan Chen and which it will hurt me to lose again.

Soon I discover pages and pages of the Oxford English Dictionary wrapped like a chrysalis around a single stanza of Rumi, and then histories of Muscovy, the combine harvester, and the *avant-garde*.

As I read them, I drop them through the nearest window, watch the wind carry each page up the empty street, a lonely boat to the port of my forgetting.

By early afternoon, having lifted and scraped the heavy top soil of bright white, I find a yellowing stratum below, in which handwritten pages occasionally surface like fossils or bits of broken pottery. Deeper still, *The Light in the Attic* and *The Wind in the Willows*, report cards, a pencil drawing of a long-dead dog.

At evening's fall I find the last sheet, stuck like a wet leaf to the carpet, and walk to a low window where, before letting go into gray and rustling light, I look down and read written there my own name.

PEP TALK

The ancient Peruvians carved an enormous hummingbird
into the desert floor, so big it could only be seen
from space, and just because somebody said
it would never fly.

I'm like that, a man made of water, standing
at the bottom of the lake,
surrounded by myself.

But never mind when there are great wings
beating silently overhead, when the humming

is too deep to hear. Last time, I rode for miles
in a '78 Plymouth with tribal plates
and a bumper sticker that reads

I break for anyone.

When I was a kid, every house on our street
was upside down. I would call to Tommy
and out the front door he would crawl,
carefully edging down aluminum siding
until he could safely drop
from an upstairs window ledge.

Poor Tommy, they never found the heart
that killed him.

But you know in the *Odyssey*, when old Ulysses goes
to Hell and sees the shade of his mother?
When he tries to hug her, his arms pass through.
Not because she's dead.
                    Because she's his mother.

Still, some of us glow in the dark.

Every single one of us glows in the light.
But no one can tell.

THE TARDY ONES

So much in childhood
comes through like the sound
of television
after bedtime, drifting
as lightly gray as volcanic ash
through the darkened house.

I thought it strange
when grown-ups spoke,
softly always, of "the late":
the late Mrs. Kelley or the late Mr. Freeman.

I wondered about these eternally
tardy people, spending their lives
like a toy boat
pulled on a string behind the steamer,
always coming to dinner
after the soup bowls
have been taken away.

I imagined them running after buses,
airplanes, and beautiful women,
in ties half a decade too fat
or too thin.

But over time I was more
and more left behind,
as crowds of people loved
joined "the late":

my grandfather,
who sat for decades,
in an arm-chair by the door,
with no particular place
to be;
an aunt punctual
as a German train;
my father.

I had thought the late
Dr. Smith must always miss
his patients,
but that was years before I learned
that the late are merely the dead,
and we are the tardy ones.

GRASS FIRE

The sudden flame springs to
in the tall grass, like a man
sitting up in bed. Just a spark
from the chainsaw and suddenly
a line of orange comes marching
over the low hill toward the house.

At the neighbor's place, we are beating
the grass with shovels, leaping from spot
to orange glowing spot,
while the fire department is over
the next hill and across the road.

This is the house of a man
who will be dead in a year,
but we don't know it
as we swing down on the flames
like we can swat out the moments,
those limitless flies of time.

ONCE ON THE AEGEAN

It was a month or two before we went
into our lives, those last tight days of school.
We sat at night upon the rocky beach
and watched the moon drift out toward Istanbul.

The sea crept up the stony stretch to make
a count of pebbles on that jagged shore,
to number underneath its waves the rocks
collected there four thousand years before.

And as we looked out at the midnight waves
a bird's cry from the dark broke in
and made the ocean lose its ancient place
and forced the sea to start the count again,
to start the ancient counting once again.

THE HOUSING SITUATION IN AMERICA

We are walking away
from the home for the elderly,
the aged in gowns and robes floating
like jellyfish in a fluorescent sea behind us,
when my wife says, *how pitiful to live
only in the past.*

Ever the contrarian, I reply
that I pity more those who live
only in the present,
such cramped apartments
in which to keep
a life:

they must constantly catch
their elbows on sharp
corners of present concerns,
pacing their low and narrow hallways
until restlessness drives
them into little back
gardens to pluck
the meager flowers of the day,

while the leisured inhabitants of time's fullness
wander into their homes through a vine-laced
and rusted back gate, coming in from the vast
and shaggy woods of history—where they have wandered
with Basho, Galileo, and Washington—to dwell in mansions
of many rooms, ramshackle but as spacious
as a top hat.

Look, now they are jumping
straight up, their arms extended overhead
as if for flight, yet they never even brush
that domed and distant ceiling.

LOSS

She carries a miniature portrait
in the pocket of her jacket,
south/southwest
of her heart,
where it bumps
above the ribcage,
a little window
the size of a salmon fillet
and framed in black walnut.

It's just the sort of thing
Sir Walter Raleigh may have carried
as an icon of his Queen.

It is painted in straw-yellow,
a field of grass with circles
of black ash settled,
like snow between dry blades.

We see only the field:
the subject of the portrait is elsewhere.

THE SUBMERGED TOWN

If a man lives
long enough, the world
he was born into becomes
a submerged town,
little places out west
where they build a lake
from a river, blocking
the stream's long conversation
into the valley.

All the buildings go
underwater. The steeple
on the clapboard church
almost breaks the surface,
but doesn't. The post office lurks
lower down, fish swimming
behind the windowed counter.
Everyone's childhood
home becomes a fishbowl castle.

And the smooth skin of the lake
stretches unbroken
within the rim of green,
as flat as Kansas,
as reflective as polished steel.

THE BOOKS OF THE DEAD

A young girl, twelve or fourteen,
one thin hand in leisurely
flight to her open mouth
is yawning in the library,

on a low couch
beside a long and sunny
window

with just the same
casualness as the voices
of the dead
speak from books.

Any morning
you might
meet your father,
the intellectual
bald from chemo, shuffling
softly in his bathrobe
through the rumpled
pages of Dostoevsky,

or that dear
old teacher,
somewhere in Virgil's
Eclogues, feet
in the brook, brown pants
rolled to knobby
knees, socks
laid out on the bank beside him.

Perhaps you have a school-friend,
still rummaging about
Das Kapital with a wrench,

and there's your Grandma,
nestled amidst the psalms,
a straw hat
left among the cabbages.

It's like returning to a broad, green place,
ringed with elms and cottonwoods,
were you picnicked with friends
a quarter century ago

to find them all still there,
taking up the plates and
pouring steaming coffee from a thermos.

You sit down and resume.

PASTORAL

It was the cool of day when God came down
to walk in Eden, as you may remember,
but with the way our sun burns grass to brown,
we won't be seeing God until December.

Still, note the way the pump jack makes a cross
in dizzy shadow on the bare of earth;
outside the gates we find another loss
in taking meager signs for little worth.

The pump jack nods above the grassy rut
and could be dipping its steel head to find
the graves of all my fresh-lost Edens, but
the plots are deeply laid within my mind,

which is another way to say the fields
are all but empty now the crew is gone:
the wild burs rush the hill, the grass yields,
the tuneless wind with rusted junk plays on.

WITH MY DAUGHTER AT THE COUNTY FAIR

I think of the costal house
where sea cliff
has rushed to meet backdoor,

of plates spinning on tall wooden sticks,
the earth's frail, falling orbit, all

precarious things, when I see you.

Daughter, when you confide
you fear your fingers are guns,

I, who have been so loud about the house,
must now will to love you louder
than any voice in your head.

Since you have had a bed,
you have been falling

from it. No matter
how I have put you down
each night, how carefully

I've arranged your small
body beneath the blanket,

I've found you at odd
angles in the old
house's bone chill,

one bare arm already
reaching for floor

like a hothouse vine in droop.
And I've put you back.

And now I watch you ride a little pirate ship,
a tilting swing back and forth on the midway.

I see you screaming through your grin,
waving to me from the arch's top,

riding the imaginary swell,
while I stand in the invisible sea,
waving back.

THE OTHER

My wife is breastfeeding our new son,
his head laid on her arm like a little farm
in the bend of a river,
a pool of white froth gathering
at the corners of his mouth.

I stand in the doorway and watch,
apostate to a rite they celebrate
beneath a single lamp,
as he squeezes her flesh and releases
in time with the throb of nourishment.

I am a man
of bronze above a plaque in the still town-square

or Caesar on the face of a buried coin,
some mute, dead temple on the back.

MANNEQUINS

All our most incessant mythology suggests
they are on the move
when we aren't
looking.

Without turning
we know
the crowds
of the faceless—
pastel polo-shirts,
white shorts,
hair a plastic suggestion—
are massing like an army
of the dead
slowly behind us

because we have seen
it in the late-night
movies we record
our dreams in.

They are a silent mob,
an underwater forest
of carnivorous plants,
inching their way toward
hapless swimmers.

You know this and are careful
not to linger
in department stores
as the last lights shudder out.

But flat on your back at night,
staring eight feet below
your ordinary ceiling,
you know also what it is
to be them:

      immobilized
in the window and gazing
across a busy avenue,
while on the opposite shore
your would-be lover stands
behind the plate glass, looking
helplessly back across
the flesh-filled street.

ORACLE

I will take my fits to be
        blessings. I will
        take my fits to be.
Blessings on the cold room
        where I take my fits
to be fitted, tailor-stitched.

But starting from an image,
        say, the fog rising
        from its earthly bed
before dawn or the dark mounds—
        fat worm volcanoes—
left in the plain and grassless dirt,

I can begin to look down
        and drag deep my brain,
        just the way drag they
the untold river for bodies,
        only the bodies
come up half-ghost, undead eyes,

and sulk on the muddy banks
        of the upper mind.
        Take this long passing—
take this passing pickup truck,
        surpassing dust cloud
raised behind the truck in dry

protest of the long, dry fact
        of passing. Or take
        this some one clear thing,
whatever it is, and get:
        the Oracle waits
in the dark woods that aren't there.

CLEAR CUTTING

Here, where our path broadens
into the middle of life, marriages begin

to fall around us like trees.
The chainsaws start up early

one morning and whine their
tedious intent into the late afternoon.

The air becomes speckled with sounds
from branches cracking against earth,

and approaching trucks jostle
the china behind its leaded glass.

Sometimes we wake at midnight
to an echo of crashing timber.

On Sundays, when the saws are silent,
we slip beneath the caution tape

and walk among the desolate stumps,
side-by-side: where Adam lost his rib,

here, our bodies barely touching.

ST. LUCY'S DAY

The neighbor has left
two large plastic bags
of dead
leaves on his lawn
for months.

One bag has a hole
from which, three
by three, leak
leaves into the wind.

And, when I think of what winter
really is—
a little more distance
from the sun—
I feel the black-cold waters
of Lethe
tugging at my ankles.

See: the eyes of the snowman are the twin
dead floating face-down in a moat around the ramparts.

Tonight the dark will be a long,
long train all night dragging
itself out of the east.

The thin house
will shudder
with its passing,

and, when dawn
finally trails in,
the puddles
around the cedar roots
will be frozen.

Driving to work,
I will see the mistletoe
hunched like vultures
in the bare scrub oaks

and roll down the window
to let in the wet stench
of grass rotting
beneath the melting snow.

A FRIEND'S DIVORCE

He has a plastic bucket by the door
for every gift she's given him:
a silver wristwatch, an old-fashioned pen,
a tie with tiny shamrocks. Things

too big for the bucket are pushed
onto the back porch, where
the leather sofa she bought
grows liver spots in the rain.

He's taken a scalpel to his brain,
gingerly slicing out matter
in the shape
of the espresso machine
from their first Christmas,
the grandfather clock
she brought home
from the junk store.

He is becoming a man who reminds
me of the famous conductor
with a brain injury, each moment
a wave of the sea. No wave knows
the wave before. Still

he is able to conduct,
memory direct from heart
to rolling, floating hand. He gives
himself wholly
to the music of half a minute
and the next doesn't know
why he is crying.

WANDERLUST

As if it started in the groin. As if
what leaves the emptied farm to fade behind
the weedy field may be what leads the self
to empty out itself in *Eros*, blind
as water, mad as smoke. The leaving is
adultery plain. I have this friend who lives
now with a second wife in Greece, where his
two children wade in Homer's sea. He gives
me glimpses of this life in postcards mailed
from places seeded white with fallen stone.
In autumn when the swaths of hay are baled
I sometimes see his wife, the ex, in town,
as overhead I hear the mourning laugh
of geese who pour themselves into the south.

TALKING TO MY RACIST FRIEND

I read somewhere that all the sunlight
smacking the earth
at any moment
weighs as much
as a cruise ship,

which makes me
wonder
how much the darkness
in this conversation
with you
must weigh:

Eight semis stacked in a pyramid
and balanced on a teacup?
The Empire State Building
sopping wet?
All the dirt in Oklahoma?

Or maybe a cruise ship
of its own,
with doe-eyed passengers
waving
dumbly from the deck
as they sail obliviously off
to kiss the sullen iceberg.

GOOD FRIDAY AT THE ALAMO

The rubber flip-flops of tourists make a sound
of polite applause for the dead.

Inside: Davey Crockett's gun in a glass box,
like the tibia of Mary Magdalene at Toulon,

and behind ropes a room with traces of mission
fresco on a wall through which the women listened.

Across the street and down the bank
a dinner party passes on a barge.

I've come here on my own, 500 miles
south of my home this Holy Week,

and in Libya a man drives his flaming car
into a line of Government soldiers.

Somewhere outside of time we all cry out
from the dark of our mouths, *Crucify Him!*

A boy and old man on the sidewalk
throw bits of tortilla to the pigeons.

There is a clatter of church bells
over stone walls. The children filter through.

Oh, tour guide, tell them we have a history
of violence. Tell them we have a history

of need.

MEMORIAL DAY

It is a long way from the war,
here where garbage trucks
nod their way up the sleepy blocks
like a small herd of buffalo.

Before dawn it's eighty degrees,
and a man sits in a lawn chair
inside the mouth of his open garage,
with a cigarette and cup of coffee.

The newspaper dropped on the cool
concrete floor spells the names
in bold print over a background of gray:
Donahue, Hinkley, Johnson, Sanchez.

Up and down the street, porch lights
grow pale under the ascending sun.

THE OLD MEN

I wake up
gasping in the black sack
of night, and they
are sitting in plain
wooden chairs
near the bed,
staring at me:

the old men,
my many previous
disappointments,
manifested now
in threadbare pajamas,
worn slippers, and foreheads
as broad and white
as a winter moon.

They shuffle behind me
to the kitchen,
where the midnight
fluorescent hangs
like spider webs in the tangle
of their thin gray hair,

and we sit
around the kitchen table,
translucent hands resting
on Formica
while I pour the milk.

I look at them,
from face to aging, faded face,
and wonder
which one I will become.

MYSTERIOUS GOD

Armadillo, snake, squirrel:
an archipelago
of carnage down the highway
in August.

The hungry birds
scatter before my hood,
like an interrupted gang
of smoking teenagers:
I'm nearing another
body erupted, a furry
Aetna across both lanes.

Yet, when I arrive,
I find only watermelon rind
flung in broken green and red
on the hot asphalt,
seeds strewn out
almost as if they could grow there.

WE EACH MUST SUFFER OUR OWN GHOST

(Aeneid 6.743)

Welcome to the ghost farm, where all my ghosts are raised in rows behind the windbreak of anorexic pines. The orphaned field undulates, a plain of unmarked graves in odd clumps of dirt, patches of weed and scruff.

At one edge the root cellar has caved in and bristles with brush cut from the right-of-way. The fence is gone, but the gate remains, dust churned up from the gravel road drifting between white iron posts.

And that old aluminum door, dropped flat in the tall grass where carrots used to grow—where now does it lead?

HANGMAN

I am becoming
visible
on the gallows.

Two *e's* have alighted
like gallows birds
on the dotted line below.

The children call out letters,

but I don't think
they will guess the word,

which is
forgiveness.

AGENT OF INFINITE REGRESSION

(Inferno 3.34-39)

Maybe you wake up
on a roving iceberg
flat on your back

amid the smell of salt
and blubber. You might
find you deserve just that.

They came in black ties
and white ties, both
sides to take you away,

double, triple, quadruple
agent of infinite regression,
no side on which to stand.

"A MOST MARVELOUS PIECE OF LUCK"

for Berryman

Death is the island that arrives
at your doorstep any old
afternoon.

In McAlester, OK, there are signs
along the highway: *Hitchhikers
may be escaped prisoners.*

You were
escaping yourself three by three.

In McAlster the sky falls
flat on meth men
cooking, cooking, cook-
ing up the meth. Death
men looking up at death
as a ball of fire,
as a long grey afternoon,
as a telephone ringing
in an empty hall,

as your bone-saw
finger in air, cutting
the hard air, making
the hard point
stick like lightning
to the falling sky.

Then you died

and proved that even standing
at dead center
of the circle you can see
in only one direction.

TWITTERING MACHINE: SELF PORTRAIT AFTER KLEE

Which bird am I, in the blue and pink blemish
spreading itself thinly before dawn?

And what's the difference
between a leg and a
shackle?

Singing straight up. Singing straight up.

I'm tied in tufts of hair,
but I like the way the wire cuts
into my toes.

Perhaps I am the bird singing back
at the bird singing straight up.

Perhaps I am the bird singing down.

I know, at least, who made the table.
I know, at least, who turns the crank.

A FAMILY

is a fence line
through tall grass,

each post
bent
by a slightly different
wind.

WHAT HAMLET GOT WRONG

That is not the undiscovered country.
We know that place well,
though we've never seen it,
like the roofs of our own
mouths. We carry it mapped
in invisible ink, and its native
grasses fall in bunches
from our pockets.

But this place is strange,
the shaggy wilderness
we stare at from a thin beach,
while the ship sails away
behind us.

DEEP FORK

after reading David Young's Du Fu

This flat river gives red back
to the sky above it,

both carrying dust and flakes
of clipped grass.

I walk with a slight limp
into the middle of my life,

watch turtles raise
their heads in dead water,

in my pocket two crumpled rejection
notes from magazines on the coast.

A tree frog near my ear
begins its whine,

and I plan to cease my argument
with God about my little life.

I've been blessed with two
plots near the edge of town

and the opportunity to live
on the face of the southern plains.

I'm going to start wearing overalls
and riding an old tractor down Maine.

I'll spend my days with these two
crows, see what it is they know.

BAD HARVEST

The roving combine crews have moved on north to Kansas,
their hulking green machines wobbling on flatbed trailers.

With little rain comes little wheat, the fields left like a dog
shaved for mange. Mornings, I sit on the porch with the paper

until the heat drives me inside. Last year there was this pretty
cashier at the Dollar General, her face round and nice, but the meth

sucked her inside out bit by bit over the year, so that
by harvest she was old paper from a wasp's nest. I'm thinking

about things that don't turn out right: it's like William Henry Harrison,
who won the "common man" with log cabin-shaped bottles

of hard cider and a reputation in war; science may tell
us his long speech in the rain and cold had nothing

to do with the pneumonia that killed him 30 days
into his term, but what does science know about disappointment?

When I was almost through with college, I crossed a lake
so red you would think only the Pentecostals could have dreamed it,

and lived for a week on the other side, painting my uncle's cabin,
refreshing the white of the trim and railings. Working under

hot glare, I would run into the murky red lake, feet slurping
through leaf rot and mud. Then one day it rained and I sat

on the porch reading Hemingway under clear plastic
sheeting. I was 23 and engaged, dumb as a bull frog,

eating chili from a can and making margaritas
from limeade and cheap tequila. I thought

I was writing a novel. Evenings I would watch the trotline
bobbers nodding into the darkness and each morning

wake beneath mosquito netting on the porch. I actually thought
I was writing a novel. Thank God it didn't turn out that way.

LENT

A scrub oak stump,
about waist high,
rises from the brown
winter grass, and my fingers
trace black scars
where last summer's fire
seared the bark and whitened
the flesh.

I'm reading
messages in braille,
continuing
past the leveled
top and up the invisible
trunk to a place
where my fingers
dance in thin sunlight
among the unseen leaves.

HAULING HAY

Over forty acres of roughly level yellow pasture
the only thing moving is a dually truck and its flatbed trailer.

From a distance, I can see the round bales heaved up
like little suns, two men lifting each star.

Overhead a vapor trail marks the passing of a jet,
a long white argument about distance and emptiness,

which leads me into thought: the spare copiousness
of the southern plains, the hay almost ex nihilo.

In a few weeks the haulers of hay will gather
at long wooden tables to give thanks—

for arms grown into heavy iron between wrist
and elbow, for fuel shaved from the scowling

face of the prairie, for almost enough rain and too much sun—
to the God who inhabits all this space in echo and in blue.

THE OIL OF MERCY

Planes moving through low air make me think of killdeer chased out of short grass, fleeing before the farm truck. I'm planted in an airport bar in St. Louis, while my father thins into a final semicolon on his hospice bed. When Adam was dying he sent Seth backwards to Eden, up the sin-singed path of the fallen foot prints, to fetch the oil of mercy. This according to the *Cursor Mundi*, which I read in a university library, at a wooden table where someone had carved *true love forever* and where I laid the large book over the carving while 465 miles away my father was cooking up a cancer like a summer storm. They would not give Seth the oil. He received, instead, three visions:

> A bare tree, limbs like chalk outlines against a winter sky

> A snake wrapped in green stripes around the trunk of the barren tree

> A baby, naked and red, caught like a balloon in the upper branches

FRENCH PRESS

Very like watching the ocean's curve
for the whale to surface,
is watching the kettle for steam.

Because our lives are impoverished
of process, I boil the water,
lay the grounds like seed in the pitcher.

And the empty cup waits
like folded hands.

KNOCK-KNOCK JOKES

This silly liturgy, common
as salt
in our bodies,
can conjure
up a door between any two
people in any place
and then open it.

I carefully teach
it to my two small daughters
one night in the tub, going
over the routine
like it was the names
of our ancestors,
a catechism of nonsense
while I work the soapy rag
between their toes:
No, you say *knock-knock*;
I'll say *who's there?*

They need
this common knowledge.
Go up to any person
on the street, any
executive, any
farmer and say
knock-knock,

and, like two
neighbors from a far
away village suddenly
met beneath city lights,
there is connection.

So much so
that, should I ever
find myself small

at the big end of a gun,
I will travel the long highway
of the barrel until I have reached
the wall that is the angry face
and seek the door that is the eye
and say *knock-knock.*

MY TEETH

I always envied the kids
with braces, their mouth
an orderly regiment in silver dress.

My teeth are a ragamuffin platoon,
Falstaff's muster;
like scandalous relatives,
I hide them away for family photos.

They met a baseball bat
once and came away
looking like a fence line
tugged hard by the years
or a row of scrub oaks
on a bald hillside.

But perhaps they are the incarnated projections of my errant thoughts,
the random distress signals of my flesh-buried skeleton,
and the secret flag of my upbringing.

When I smile in the mirror,
they are a small congregation
of drunks, leaning
against invisible
strangers who might
be guardian angels.

A LOVE SUPREME

I can't think
of anything
else: that rhythm
like a holy
ghost jungle
cat stalking
behind a line
of trees at dusk.

I've got no
right, white
and rural,
to feel
about it like this,

but, yes, when
the incense
of that sax
starts twisting
up toward heaven,
my soul,
like a little
brother, comes
running behind,
shouting,
"I'm coming too!"
and tripping
on its shoelaces.

AN URGENT MESSAGE TO LI PO

Look, I say, the snow is falling
on our shoulders and hair.
But you say perhaps we
are a thing that is happening
to the snow.

CLASS OUTSIDE

It's never as good as students think
it will be: even in Arcadia
weed-whackers whine
in a hover above our voices.

The professor gets grass
stains on his khaki seat,
and half the class is gone
when a girl in white shorts walks by.

Even when it kind of works, the wind
keeps turning pages, a mosquito
gets smeared across the *Georgics*,
a ladybug lands in someone's tea.

But every spring we are back
out here on the grass, ringed
on the green, posing
for university photographers,

and squinting to read in the glare
of the sun's brand new flesh.

CALL OUT MY NAME

and it comes running,
a dog shaggy with consonants,
little but burly and quick.
You will notice how it pulls
the short leash behind,
by which it drags
into your presence
all that I am.

LAST WORDS

Lady Death, when she walks
in wearing her black
evening dress,
pearls like a string
of islands around her slender neck,
will find me
as awkward as always
with women.

Maybe, if I go slow,
a long chain of pale afternoons
like my father
dwindling in his cancer,
I'll be prepared;

but if death comes
sudden as headlights
around a dark curve,
I will surely only muster
the heavy lump of the obvious:
it's a train!
or
watch out for those zombies!
or
my heart!

I would prefer to stand
mute before the hungry
door and listen, as I go:

the distant drone of a lawn mower;
the 5:30 carpool honking from the driveway;
the pub where clinking dinnerware
echoes down a dim brick street.

I would hear the birds
singing neither
elegy nor so long.

Better that than waste
my last moments batting
after eloquence like a cat
after a June-bug

or, worse, end up hanging
around some Ouija board,
endlessly revising.

THE MAN FROM THE COLONIES

It's always the Roman Empire in outer space,
where men in gold lamé togas are oppressing the natives

of some planet on the outer rim. On one of those planets
it's 1988, and I am fourteen years old and it's snowing

like Hell. My parents have bought my big sister
an old car for Christmas and hidden it behind the barn.

I've got to start it each morning in the corpse-black
cold, or the engine will fall forever into the silence

around us. I sit behind the wheel, blowing warm moisture
from my lungs like smoke from my father's Kools

while I let the engine ramble on about something
to do with clanking and grinding, the radio

tuned to a college station out of Dallas. I'm imagining
what would happen if I yanked the column stick

down and rolled, wind sauntering in through
the windows warmer and warmer as I drift further

south, everything I know balled and frozen into an iceberg
drifting away behind me. And then I'm nearly forty.

When I crawl out my window onto the roof
of the new house on this planet on the edge

of a vast and lecherous empire, I can see the barn
behind the house where I grew up. All the dogs

in town begin to bark, asking me why
I never went anywhere, and I see versions

of my childhood friends walking up and down the sidewalk.
We are like a grassy field worn thin with the passing

of cattle. Some evenings on this far-flung planet I drive
my two daughters out to the house where I grew up

and sit in the minivan with the engine idling. At night
I sleep beside the wife of my youth, her breathing

settling over everything like that snow from long ago.
That's when I know I want to die on this other earth

and will ask her to bury me in its hard, metallic dirt,
so that the seeds of my bones don't sprout too quickly

and so that the folks in Heaven will know which way
to watch for me to come walking.

IN THE GRAVEYARD I MEET ANOTHER JOGGER

Gravestones perch like egrets and crows
on a grassy hill overlooking our little town,

as if the rare rain were meant
to wash the dead back down over the living.

We are running through this place in thin hope
of staying out of it a little longer. We know

it won't work, remember the eighteen-year-old
athlete whose heart burst at half court, the young

teacher struck by lightning in the door
of the schoolhouse. That is why we laugh

lightly as we pass from opposite directions:
the mirth of mutual futility. My legs are ringing

like the bells of Notre Dame from the uphill
climb to the cemetery. There is a little league game

over the low fence and across the road; without
my glasses, eyes full of sweat, I mistake the blue

and white shapes for more stones, until they break
into motion. On the other side of the grounds

the plots peter out, one and two, until there is
only empty grass stretching to a back fence

holding the tide of scrub oak and cedar.
There is room. I'll meet you here again.

May it be many years from now.

coda

Your whole life now must be one of longing, if you are to achieve perfection. And this longing must be in the depths of your will, put there by God, with your consent.

The Cloud of Unknowing

NOTES FROM A TIME TRAVELER

1.

My dear,
I've landed back in Paris.
The year is 1865, our own.
I thought you were to meet me here.
It rained all day. I watched the hats
of merchants float like barges up
and down a rain-drenched street. I'm waiting
in rooms I've taken in the house
kept by the owl-faced matron. Come. Come soon.
Until you do, I will remain
                              your sorrowing,
                                    Pascal

2.

My dear,
it seems you will not come
to Paris, so arrangements have been made.
I will depart for Rome next week.
I shall be glad to leave the noise of much
construction, as they build and build
this city every day. I'll land
in Rome for its decline, which now
begins to suit my mood. I am
                              still yours,
                                    Pascal

3.

Dearest,
it is better here in Rome, though I've somehow missed
my mark, arriving in the reign of Caracalla.

They say the Emperor has gone into the East. There are smiths
nearby; I hear the hammers murmur through the afternoon.

My accommodations are cheap and dirty, jutting
over the street like the chin of a beggar.

I fear the structure may collapse and spend little time at home.
Most days I pour myself into the throbbing crowds,

but this afternoon I walked alone through that olive orchard, where we
used to walk. But that was a century later, perhaps more,

although I thought I saw you in the shade, washing your ankles
in the little stream between the trees.

It was only the yellow-haired girl kept by the orchard master.
Tomorrow I shall see about a guide for the Etruscan tombs.

I'll wait before I see the gardens of Sallust again. I am tormented
by your delay, but I remain
                          your devoted,
                                    Pascal

4.

Dearest,
Entswhistle tells me you are
in Cordova, though he doesn't know
the year. I wonder if these notes
even reach you. Without word
I shall make a guess and come.

                              Pascal

5.

My dear,
I waited long in Spain, but you
did not appear. To what can I compare
you? Once, when I was small, my father took
me walking through the countryside. At noon
we came to poplars on a grassy bank,
their shade a bridge across the little stream,
and he laid down to sleep awhile. But I
was wide awake and wandered to the edge.
Beneath the water's dream I saw a stone
bright red among the other stones. I reached
and fell. The sunlight shattered all around
and then a voice above the stream. He pulled
me out.

        Should you decide to come to me,
I am in England with the Virgin Queen.

6.

My dearest one,
forgive my mood last note.
The plague has come like blizzard on the town.
They do not know it is the rats and shut
themselves in sickened rooms to die. I feel
a fever coming on and shall remove
myself for better care elsewhere. For now,
know still I am a leaf adrift upon
your flood, a rumor of a distant city
burning, a basement room below the house
of all your thoughts, and yet still yours,

                                        Pascal

7.

Fever. Burning. L.A., 1981. The men in white masks were out and
in all day, asking about my mother. They will not catch her: she's
a balloon and may pop. You have a lover. There are spider-webs as
thick as quilts upon the ceiling here, but only mechanical spiders
like at the world's fair Paris where you held my hand and where we
heard the man on the phonograph. I heard your voice behind the
television. Do you have a lover? Remember the olive grove. But was
it your arms or was it the Tiber? Tiger. They say the ones closest to
the bombs will become the air they stand in. They've put a tube in
my arm or else they've pulled my veins external. You are the air I
stand in. Do these notes reach you? They add more blankets each
day. P.

8.

My dear,
my fever never broke but drained
itself while I was sleeping. Now I see
the truth about the two of us. This room
is all linoleum and white. The light
pokes its thin fingers into everything.
This is a place where it is hard to not
see. You do not love me, and I will go
beyond the edges of our time. Do not
expect much more from me. I will leave you
a note or two, like bats to call my darkness.
Farewell, my love and greatest wound.

                                    Pascal

9.

Again I come to the sun's expanding phase, as the seas begin to rise

        into the air, lifting themselves *en masse* with a hiss.

This day of ash, this last day, I am again looking

        and looking for the pomegranate seed that will keep

me below the ground. Again the terrible Spring. Many times

        I repeat this day, more like an incessant nod than a refrain.

The trees are removing their wide green hats

to relieve their burning scalps. The window glass is melting.

I have sat down with the blossoming dead

and will sit with them this day again tomorrow.

10.

My dear,
I've seen both ends of time and say
nothing. As it was in the beginning,
it is now and ever shall be. Nothing
has changed between the two of us, but still
I hope. A horse's feet are knocking past
on stone below my window, going on.
Each morning there is coffee with the news
from home. In afternoon I watch the smoke
pool up around the church's tile roof.
I know you will not come and yet I wait
in France, where I remain the fool,

Pascal.

CPSIA information can be obtained at www.ICGtesting.com
Printed in the USA
LVOW07s1426130815

449997LV00006B/208/P